WHOLESOME CHILDREN'S BOOKS

SAMEER KOCHURE

Copyright © 2025 by Sameer Kochure.

All rights reserved. No part of this publication may be reproduced, distributed or transmitted in any form or by any means, including photocopying, recording, or other electronic or mechanical methods, without the prior written permission of the publisher, except in the case of brief quotations embodied in critical reviews and certain other noncommercial uses permitted by copyright law. For permission requests, write to the publisher at the address below.

Sameer Kochure,
P2-37, DEC Towers, Al Seba Street,
Dubai Marina, Dubai, UAE.

email(@)sameerkochure(.)com

Publisher's Note: This is a work of fiction. Names, characters, places, concepts, and ideas are a product of the author's imagination. Locales and public names are sometimes used for atmospheric purposes. Any resemblance to actual people, living or dead, or to businesses, companies, events, institutions, or locales is completely coincidental.

'Dude, you are going to poop...' by Sameer Kochure — First Edition.

THIS BOOK BELONGS TO

_____

DEDICATED TO MY MUM, AND YOUR MUM,
AND ALL OUR MUMS, AND TO EVERYONE WE LOVE,
AND TO EVERYONE WHO LOVES US.

BUT THIS HOME-PLANET OF OURS IS A LITTLE RUBBER BALL,

Learn to Laugh at the Lightning and Dance with the Rain...

ALSO BY SAMEER KOCHURE

* * *

WHOLESOME CHILDREN'S BOOKS

Dude, you are going to poop! (Body positivity)

My dear Princess, you are going to fart! (Body positivity)

Look up at the wonders, kiddo! (Digital screen detox)

Where do they go... (Separation anxiety)

When mamma and dadda go mad... (Arguing adults)

Bullies are like balloons... (Coping with bullying)

* * *

Exclusive bundle deals available on the official author website
www.sameerkochure.com

ALSO BY SAMEER KOCHURE

* * *

YOUNG ADULT COMFORT-READ BOOKS

A Young Boy And His Best Friend, The Universe — Volumes 1–10.
Comfort-read short stories that answer life's toughest questions—including the ones keeping you up at night.

The Tiny Fireball
A cute, wholesome, comfort-read sci-fi fantasy featuring star-crossed lovers.

* * *

HEALING POETRY BOOKS FOR GROWNUPS

Made of Flowers and Steel
An empowering poetry collection that celebrates the raw grit and inner strength of women.

Tough Skins, Tender Hearts
Poems about men, for everyone who loves them.

Wrong.
An inspiring poetry collection.

* * *

Exclusive bundle deals available on the official author website:
www.sameerkochure.com

www.ingramcontent.com/pod-product-compliance
Lightning Source LLC
LaVergne TN
LVHW071322080526
838199LV00080B/717